Teacher's Guide

Classroom Worksheets

Restart

By:

David Lee

Classroom Worksheets and Activities is a series of books designed to provide teachers ready to use activities with students. The focus of this book is to provide student focused material. Information evaluating, labeling and discussing the text will not be presented in this series.

This includes several labeled graphic organizers and advice on how to use them in the classroom. Several of these organizers can be used for assessment.

Teaching Suggestions

Characters

Chase Ambrose

Shoshanna Weber

Principal

Dr. Fitzwallace

Brendan Esponoza

Helene

Mom

Dad

Aaron Hakimian

Bear

Hugo

Kimberly Tooley

Joel Weber

Ms. Deleo

Julius Solway

Teaching Suggestions

<u>Themes and Topics</u>

Bully

Amnesia

Forgiveness

Friendship

Teaching Suggestions

Start With The prereading Questions. (individual Activity)

Use the Chapter/Page Summary (individual or group activity)

Advertisement—Only necessary when text presents an important item

Chapter to Poem—Good for end of text review

Character Sketch—Provide at the introduction of a new character, continue to edit and revise as the novel continues to develop

Comic Strip— Good for summarizing a small summary of the novel

Compare and Contrast—Use with places, characters, times, and themes

Create the Test—Pick the best ones to use for cumulative exam

Draw the Scene—Alternative chapter view option

Interview— Good for practicing voice

Lost Scene—Helps provide connections between sections of a text

Making Connections—Good for cumulative review of main ideas

Precognition Sheet—Use during the middle

Activity Descriptions

Research Connection—Use when historical context is needed to fully understand the text

Sequencing—Use to help establish the order of a series of actions, middle to end review

Travel Brochure—Use to help develop awareness of location

Top Ten List—Good for review

Vocabulary Box—Use the chapter/page summary to help identify vocabulary lists

Who, What, When, Where, and How—Variation of the create the test

Props Needed— Helps with establishing location

Activity Descriptions

Advertisement—Select an item from the text and have the students use text clues to draw an advertisement about that item.

Chapter to Poem—Students select 20 words from the text to write a five line poem with 3 words on each line.

Character Sketch—Students complete the information about a character using text clues.

Comic Strip— Students will create a visual representation of the chapter in a series of drawings.

Compare and Contrast—Select two items to make relationship connections with text support.

Create the Test—have the students use the text to create appropriate test questions.

Draw the Scene—students use text clues to draw a visual representation of the chapter.

Interview— Students design questions you would ask a character in the book and then write that characters response.

Lost Scene—Students use text clues to decide what would happen after a certain place in the story.

Making Connections—students use the text to find two items that are connected and label what kind of relationship connects them.

Precognition Sheet—students envision a character, think about what will happen next, and then determine what the result of that would be.

Activity Descriptions

Pyramid—Students use the text to arrange a series of items in an hierarchy format.

Research Connection—Students use an outside source to learn more about a topic in the text.

Sequencing—students will arrange events in the text in order given a specific context.

Support This! - Students use text to support a specific idea or concept.

Travel Brochure—Students use information in the text to create an informational text about the location

Top Ten List—Students create a list of items ranked from 1 to 10 with a specific theme.

Vocabulary Box—Students explore certain vocabulary words used in the text.

What Would You Do? - Students compare how characters in the text would react and compare that with how they personally would react.

Who, What, When, Where, and How—Students create a series of questions that begin with the following words that are connected to the text.

Write a Letter—Students write a letter to a character in the text.

Activity Descriptions (for scripts and poems)

Add a Character—Students will add a character that does not appear in the scene and create dialog and responses from other characters.

Costume Design—Students will design costumes that are appropriate to the characters in the scene and explain why they chose the design.

Props Needed— Students will make a list of props they believe are needed and justify their choices with text.

Soundtrack! - Students will create a sound track they believe fits the play and justify each song choice.

Stage Directions— Students will decide how the characters should move on, around, or off stage.

Poetry Analysis—Students will determine the plot, theme, setting, subject, tone and important words and phrases.

Before Reading Questions

What is the reason for reading this book?

What do you already know about this book?

What, based on the cover, do you think this book is about?

Before Reading Questions

Have you read any other books by this author?

Is this book part of a series? If so what are the other books?

What are you looking forward to when reading this book?

NAME:

TEACHER:

Date:

Chapters/Pages

Events

1.

2.

3.

4.

5.

* <u>Not all number lines will have answers.</u>

Characters

1.

2.

3.

4.

5.

6.

Possible Future Events

1.

2.

Locations

1.

2.

Key Terms / Vocabulary

1.

2.

3.

4.

Conflicts / Problems

1.

2.

3.

4.

Main Idea

After Reading Questions

What parts of the book were the most enjoyable?

Which characters were your favorite and why?

Write a summary of the book.

After Reading Questions

What are the 5 most important events?

Write a review of the book.

What is likely to be a plot to the next book?

NAME:

TEACHER:

Date:

Advertisement: Draw an advertisement for the book

NAME:

TEACHER:

Date:

Chapter to Poem

Assignment: Select 20 words found in the chapter to create a poem where each line is 3 words long.

Title:

_____   _____   _____

_____   _____   _____

_____   _____   _____

_____   _____   _____

_____   _____   _____

NAME:

TEACHER:

Date:

Character Sketch

Name

Draw a picture

Personality/ Distinguishing marks

Connections to other characters

Important Actions

NAME:

TEACHER:

Date:

Comic Strip

Compare and Contrast

Venn Diagram

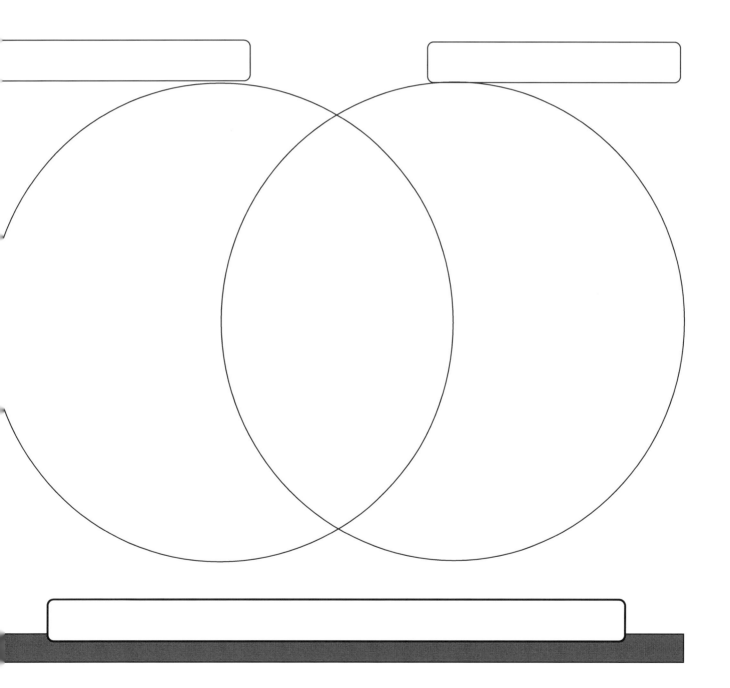

NAME:

TEACHER:

Date:

Create the Test

Question:

Answer:

Question:

Answer:

Question:

Answer:

Question:

Answer:

NAME:

TEACHER:

Date:

Draw the Scene: What five things have you included in the scene?

1

2

3

4

5

NAME:

TEACHER:

Date:

Interview: Who _____

Question:

Answer:

Question:

Answer:

Question:

Answer:

Question:

Answer:

NAME:

TEACHER:

Date:

Lost Scene: Write a scene that takes place between _____ and

_____

Making Connections

What is the connection?

NAME:

TEACHER:

Date:

Precognition Sheet

Who ?

What's going to happen?

What will be the result?

Who ?

What's going to happen?

What will be the result?

Who ?

What's going to happen?

What will be the result?

Who ?

What's going to happen?

What will be the result?

How many did you get correct?

NAME:

TEACHER:

Date:

Assignment: Pyramid

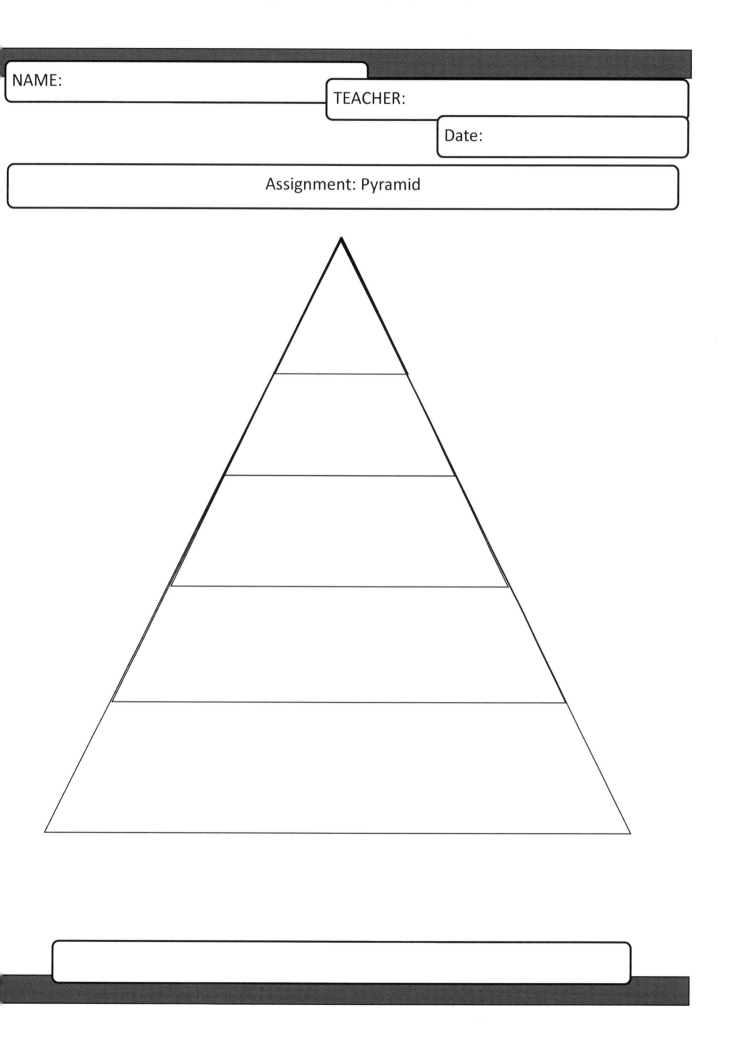

NAME:

TEACHER:

Date:

Research connections

Source (URL, Book, Magazine, Interview)

What am I researching?

Facts I found that could be useful or notes

1.

2.

3.

4.

5.

6.

NAME:

TEACHER:

Date:

Sequencing or timeline

1.

2.

3.

4.

5.

NAME:

TEACHER:

Date:

Support This!

Supporting text

What page?

Supporting text

What page?

Central idea or statement

Supporting text

What page?

Supporting text

What page?

Travel Brochure

Why should you visit?

What are you going to see?

Map

Special Events

NAME:

TEACHER:

Date:

Top Ten List

1.

2.

3.

4.

5.

6.

7.

8.

9.

10.

Vocabulary Box

Definition:

Draw:

Word:

Related words:

Use in a sentence:

Definition:

Draw:

Word:

Related words:

Use in a sentence:

NAME:

TEACHER:

Date:

What would you do?

Character: _____

What did they do?

Example from text:

What would you do?

Why would that be better?

Character: _____

What did they do?

Example from text:

What would you do?

Why would that be better?

Character: _____

What did they do?

Example from text:

What would you do?

Why would that be better?

NAME:

TEACHER:

Date:

Who, What, When, Where, and How

Who

What

Where

When

How

NAME:

Write a letter

To:

From:

NAME:

TEACHER:

Date:

Assignment:

NAME:

TEACHER:

Date:

Add a Character

Who is the new character?

What reason does the new character have for being there?

Write a dialog between the new character and characters currently in the scene.

You dialog must be 6 lines or more, and can occur in the beginning, middle or end of the scene.

NAME:

TEACHER:

Date:

Costume Design

Draw a costume for one the characters in the scene.

Why do you believe this character should have a costume like this?

NAME:

TEACHER:

Date:

Props Needed

Prop:

What text from the scene supports this?

Prop:

What text from the scene supports this?

Prop:

What text from the scene supports this?

NAME:

TEACHER:

Date:

Soundtrack!

Song:

Why should this song be used?

Song:

Why should this song be used?

Song:

Why should this song be used?

NAME:

TEACHER:

Date:

Stage Directions

List who is moving, how they are moving and use text from the dialog to determine when they move.

Who:

How:

When:

Who:

How:

When:

Who:

How:

When:

NAME:

TEACHER:

Poetry Analysis

Date:

Name of Poem:

Subject:

Text Support:

Plot:

Text Support:

Theme:

Text Support:

Setting:

Text Support:

Tone:

Text Support:

Important Words and Phrases:

Why are these words and phrases important:

Made in United States
Orlando, FL
15 July 2022

19845390R00043